T0114617

SIMPLE, EASY TRANSFORMATION

How to forgive ourselves and others and live a happy life

ZO HOUSEMAN

BALBOA.PRESS

A DIVISION OF HAY HOUSE

Copyright © 2023 Zo Houseman.

All rights reserved. No part of this book may be used or reproduced by
any means, graphic, electronic, or mechanical, including photocopying,
recording, taping or by any information storage retrieval system
without the written permission of the author except in the case of
brief quotations embodied in critical articles and reviews.

Balboa Press books may be ordered through booksellers or by contacting:

Balboa Press
A Division of Hay House
1663 Liberty Drive
Bloomington, IN 47403
www.balboapress.com
844-682-1282

Because of the dynamic nature of the Internet, any web addresses or
links contained in this book may have changed since publication and
may no longer be valid. The views expressed in this work are solely those
of the author and do not necessarily reflect the views of the publisher,
and the publisher hereby disclaims any responsibility for them.

The author of this book does not dispense medical advice or prescribe the use
of any technique as a form of treatment for physical, emotional, or medical
problems without the advice of a physician, either directly or indirectly. The
intent of the author is only to offer information of a general nature to help
you in your quest for emotional and spiritual well-being. In the event you use
any of the information in this book for yourself, which is your constitutional
right, the author and the publisher assume no responsibility for your actions.

Any people depicted in stock imagery provided by Getty Images are
models, and such images are being used for illustrative purposes only.
Certain stock imagery © Getty Images.

ZoHouseman.com

Print information available on the last page.

ISBN: 979-8-7652-4523-1 (sc)
ISBN: 979-8-7652-4522-4 (e)

Library of Congress Control Number: 2023917138

Balboa Press rev. date: 10/11/2023

To all who have chosen to be embodied on the planet at this great and auspicious time:

The courage to let go of the emotional baggage we have collected along the way and to arrive at peace and freedom is to be celebrated and honored.

This book is dedicated to us all.

Contents

Preface

THIS BOOK WAS INSPIRED BY a question posed to me by a friend. "Zo," she said, "if you were to leave the planet today, what would you want the world, the planet, and the people to see and know?" This book is the answer to that question.

We all have the ability to change our lives and the course of the planet. It's an inside job. We can change our thoughts and ideas around how we view this world and our lives. We can create peace, love, joy, wisdom, and understanding.

How? Simply by changing how we think and feel about ourselves and the world around us. All we need to do is forgive ourselves and others for our errors in thinking.

When Jesus said, "Rise up and walk and 'sin' no more," he was saying, "Go, and err no more." The word translated into English as "sin" was *hamartia*, a term of archery that originally meant "a miss of the mark"—not hitting the bull's-eye—and hence an error or fault in general, a "sin." I believe he was saying "Go and err no more" so they didn't draw back into the thoughts that created the malady they were suffering from in the first place. We also have the opportunity to let go of our errors in thinking through forgiveness and go and live the life we have been waiting for.

We don't all have to agree on everything; we just need to give ourselves permission to allow ourselves and others to have their own perceptions and not take it personally. We can do that by realizing that nothing is real, so why would we want to get all excited and irritated about it? The emotions we feel are combined with the thoughts we are having to create all the difficulties we experience in the here and now. If we could curb our emotions, we would be a lot more rational in our responses. One way to unwind our reactions is to forgive ourselves for the beliefs we cling to and make peace within our own system.

This book is a way to forgive ourselves and others and calm our emotional responses to the world around us. It includes a new revision of my 2005 book, *100 Minutes to Happiness*.

To all who assisted me in waking up and remembering who I am: I acknowledge you and myself for finding our way to a better life. Special thanks to Anna, Blair, Drue, James, Nita, Rebecca, Sandy, Lila, Cathy, Elaine, Sally, Deb, Janeen, and Alicia Rose for all their input and support.

Introduction

I STARTED THIS PROCESS BY TAKING one thought at a time and writing out pages and pages of sentences beginning *When you did this, I felt* ... . Then I would write out all the feelings and reactions I had to the person or situation. Next I wrote a forgiveness statement to the offender, and also to myself for the part I had played. I would ask for help in releasing myself and the other from blame.

The next step was to write out a positive statement to replace the old pattern. I wrote on Post-it Super Sticky Notes that I placed where I would see them several times daily. The statement eventually became "programmed" into my mind. This process of integrating the new thought would take a couple weeks, and then the next thought started niggling at me, and I would repeat the process. Well, this was taking a lot of time! I thought there must be a faster way, and I thought about it quite often.

As time went on, I learned how to shift the negative thoughts I was having about myself and others in a more efficient way and still move the energy quicker and easier. A few years ago, a friend told me about a book called *The Emotion Code* by Dr. Bradley Nelson. I read the book, and the system it outlined was basically what I had been doing, except that Dr. Nelson used a list of descriptive, emotion-related words to identify what needed to be released. (He also used the systems of the body, but I only used the emotion list.) It was a shortcut to identifying the emotions that needed to shift.

I expanded on the list of emotion-related words and used kinesiology testing to identify which emotions were involved and which of these were ready to release. Instead of having to sit with a client and dig out the core issue, I could simply use muscle testing to identify the emotion that needed to be released, and the client didn't have to talk about the issue or get emotional unless they wanted to. That made the process even simpler and faster, but it was still practitioner-dependent.

Now I have found a simple way that individuals can do the work themselves, and I am happy to share it with you.

I

HOW THIS WORKS

OUR THOUGHTS ARE THE CREATIVE force that forms the lives we are living. In order to change our lives, we can direct our thoughts consciously and create a more enjoyable experience. We are creating our lives in every moment of every day. If we can learn how to delete the thoughts that are making life feel hard and then input new thoughts, we can change our experience and have fun along the way.

Life is a series of emotion-driven stories that create the illusions we believe we are experiencing. Most of the time we feel like things are happening to us instead of understanding that our thoughts and intentions are the actual cause of what we are experiencing. If we take responsibility for the stories we have made up collectively and individually, we can change our lives. If we created it, we can uncreate it. Anything we are not happy with we can change. We create limitation, excitement, boredom … life is a series of stories. We are all innocent children playing in the energy of thought. This is key to remember when we are caught up in the emotion of our creations. God within us is having a heyday no matter what we have created. We aren't doing it wrong; it's just that we can let go of what is not working for us and exchange it for a more peaceful and calm existence, if we desire to.

I started this process in the year 2000, and at that time it was tedious. Through the years I have simplified it over and over again. Now we don't have to labor so hard to accomplish it. The energy has lightened up, and we are able to change what we are saying to ourselves in a much faster and easier way.

The first part of the process is to delete the negative thoughts we have programmed into our mind through forgiveness, and the second part is to reprogram a more positive thought to replace the old one. Statements beginning "Thanks in advance for" reprogram the deleted thoughts in this second part. If we understand and believe that we can ask for what we desire and get it, we will experience what we are asking for. It's that simple.

All that is really required is to trust that each and every one of us is hooked up to Source energy—God, the Universe, or whatever your belief system is—and that we are the conduit that energy runs through. Our thoughts are energy, and that energy is creative. We are able to direct this energy ourselves. Trusting that this is true is all we need to delete and let go of past traumas, disappointments, or other negative thoughts. Then we ask to bring in what we desire. We can also use this process to gain the trust we need to accomplish changing our minds.

The information that I am offering doesn't have to be used exactly how it's outlined or in a certain order. Read through it and start wherever you feel compelled to. You are welcome to use this however it feels correct for you. At the end of the book, I have provided pages you may use for journaling your two-step process.

2

GETTING STARTED

IF TRUSTING THAT WE ARE the conduit and are hooked up to the Creator (Source, God, the Universe …) feels difficult, here's a way to change that.

Write down "I forgive myself for believing I am separate from the Creator and have forgotten that each of us is fully and completely hooked up to Source energy, God, the Universe" (whatever your belief system is). If you need to write out more ways to forgive the error in your thinking, do that.

Sit a bit with what you wrote and let it sink in. Then write "Thanks in advance for knowing that I am a conduit of Source energy, God, the Universe," whatever your belief system is, "and I am able to delete the old thought patterns and bring in the new thoughts and ideas that are beneficial for me."

It's helpful to write out the "Thanks in advance for" on Super Sticky Notes and place them where you will see them several times per day. I like to stick them on the bathroom mirror, my day planner, in the car, and anywhere I will see them during the day. Seeing the new thought multiple times per day reinforces the new idea and integrates it faster. I focus on one Thanks in Advance statement at a time, and then when that is completed I move on to the next old pattern I wish to change. A screen saver would be good too, if you know how to do that.

A simple way to delete thoughts that are not in alignment with what we would like to experience is to use forgiveness. Sometimes we resist forgiving people we feel have wronged us. If this is true for you, do the following exercise.

Write out "I forgive myself for resisting forgiving people in my life who I believe have wronged me." You can expand on this by writing out any other thoughts you have around forgiving others.

Sit with that thought for a bit until it sinks in. Then write "Thanks in advance for opening me up to forgiveness of myself and others." Use the sticky note reminders to speed up the integration time and move on to the next item.

In the next section, we'll be looking at a great shortcut to release 50 percent of the baggage we are carrying around—without even having to know what is being let go.

3

100 MINUTES TO HAPPINESS

Be the happiness that you seek.

I FIRST WROTE ABOUT THE 100 minutes technique in 2005 as a quick and easy way to let go of the unconscious thoughts we are living by, without needing to identify the individual thoughts. It takes ten minutes a day for ten days to complete, allowing you to speed up the process and then continue on to more specific, identifiable thoughts you desire to let go of.

In 1998, at the age of forty-two, I was newly divorced and raising my two boys, aged seventeen and fourteen. We lived on the north coast of Oregon. Unbeknownst to me, in June of that year an almost mystical, magical chain of events was about to occur, ending in the split up and end of my eleven-year marriage. I know that we could say every step we take from birth leads us to where we are, but this chapter in my life started when I was thirty-nine. I tend to be a little stubborn, or at least I feel like I don't give up easily, but at that point in my life, it seemed that no matter how many times or how hard I tried, I couldn't pull my life together. I felt unhappy and defeated.

Right before the end of the marriage, I remember telling my youngest son that I didn't think I could take one more thing. I had survived and sucked up my emotions as long as I could. I was at a breaking point. My husband and I went to counseling, and the therapist dismissed my part of the dysfunction as "codependence." I had never heard that term before. I said nothing to her but decided to look it up and see what information I could find.

One day I was at Kaiser Hospital, waiting for a friend of mine, and started browsing the very limited library of books, among which I saw *Codependent No More* by Melody Beattie. I read the jacket and cover, and then put it back because she said codependent people were manipulative and controlling. I thought, *I'm nice and kind. That couldn't be about me.* Later, when a friend from Seattle asked if I had bought the book yet, I told her I didn't think I was codependent. "Zo, get the book!" she said, and took me to the bookstore to buy it. I am so glad she did! After reading the book and using Beattie's companion book *The Language of Letting Go*, I felt like the weight of the world had been lifted off my shoulders. I realized I could have been the poster child for codependency. Now I had a much better chance of being in a healthy relationship.

As I expanded personally, I kept thinking, *There must be a simpler, easier way to create a happy and peaceful life.* I have always kept this thought in mind and looked for any clues on how to do this. In time, I found a fundamental, universal pathway to self-love and happiness that anyone can follow.

Two years after my divorce, another series of seemingly random events compelled me to read and integrate into my system a vast amount of spiritual information. It seemed I was on an accelerated journey to finding and reclaiming my authentic self. I read books about self-awareness and letting go of old thoughts that irritated me, but I learned how to integrate new thoughts to assist me in creating the life I desired. This was my pathway to freedom.

One evening while I was bathing, I was inspired to combine three different systems of thought into one. Integration of these affirmations, I realized, would clear out about half the "baggage" that we aren't even conscious of, so that we begin to feel more peaceful and therefore happier in our lives without needing to know what we are letting go of. So, this is my offering to all who are ready, willing, and able. Say these affirmations two to three times a day for ten days, out loud to yourself in front of a mirror. What could be easier?

4

THOUGHTS RULE

WE ARE AN ACCUMULATION OF all the thoughts we have ever had and of every choice and every agreement we've ever made. Our logical mind does all the interpreting. If we change our thoughts, we can change everything.

We grow up a certain way. We learn to survive in the world according to our mind's ideas about life. We access information externally through our senses or internally through our feelings. In the first years of our lives, we encode a lot of information, interpreting the external world according to our experiences and coupling them with our feelings.

All the thoughts we input become our individual belief systems. The process goes like this: We have an experience. We see an event as it occurs. We hear other people's ideas about it and consider their opinions. We associate a specific feeling with the event. We come to a logical decision about what happened and couple it with the feelings we had. Using all this information, we create our interpretation of the event. We input it into our minds and live by the results of that evaluation for the rest of our lives, unless we become aware of what we decided in that moment and change it. The feelings remain the same. But we can change the interpretation and give new meaning to a particular way we are feeling.

Let's say that when you see yourself in the mirror, you have programmed in the story that you are overweight, look terrible in your clothes, and nobody likes you because you do not look the way you think you should. These thoughts were programmed into you a long time ago. You can continue to have this interpretation, but you also have the opportunity to delete these thoughts and replace them with those that will help you.

A lot of the thoughts we pattern in start occurring when we are five to seven years old. We are doing the best we can with our child brains and ability to reason to interpret the experiences that come at us. However, we are not developed enough to process some of the upsets and traumas in a healthy way. A lot of our unconscious thoughts and reactions were set in place using our limited ability to think. We are living by rules that were set up by a juvenile mind.

Do we still want to live by ideas we formed as a child? In the moment of their inception, these interpretations seemed perfectly logical to believe, but we have the ability to reassess and create new ones that will replace outdated information. You no longer need to hold on to the old thoughts that keep you stuck. You can use all the information you have gained over the years to create new thoughts and beliefs, which result in a new outlook on life.

5

A SIMPLE SYSTEM

WITH ONE AFFIRMATION AND ONE realization at a time, I clawed my way out of the gutter of negative thinking over the course of several years. As I did so, I kept thinking there must be a simpler way to do this without rehashing a person's past and entire thought system. By using specific language, there is an easier way.

The affirmations I present here cover the foundational areas of life. They address the mind, body, emotions, soul, following your heart, honoring the elemental world we live in, and being grateful for all we have. Although they're simple, they work.

I believe nearly everyone who completes this exercise—saying these affirmations for ten days, two to three times per day—will enrich their lives by 50 percent. You will feel twice as happy and peaceful as you do now. What do you have to lose? It takes less than ten minutes for ten days—100 minutes to happiness.

This easy system has four parts:

1. affirmations;
2. a brief explanation behind each affirmation;
3. feedback;
4. more thoughts and ideas that may assist you.

6

AFFIRMATIONS

YOU CAN WRITE OUT THE affirmations listed on the following page on paper or sticky notes, or photocopy the page as many times as you like. Post them on your bathroom mirror and say them out loud two to three times each day while you're doing your daily routine. It's important to look at yourself in the mirror as you're saying these affirmations out loud. If it feels more comfortable to you, you may change the wording slightly.

After ten days, these thoughts will be integrated into your mind, body, and soul. If you desire to do more with your life afterward, go for it. If not, enjoy your life right where you are!

You may want to expand this process to other aspects of your life, such as personal relationships, raising children, finding and following your passion, family relationships, or money.

Speaking to your mirror, say the following out loud two to three times a day for ten days:

- I love you.
- I love my body.
- I forgive myself for the thoughts I live by that do not help me; I release them now.
- I forgive others for their thoughts and allow them to think whatever they desire.
- I trust myself to know who I am.
- I do what pleases me in all areas of my life.
- I live my life completely, and I am grateful for being here.

Zo Houseman

7

THE AFFIRMATIONS EXPLAINED

LET'S LOOK AT WHAT EACH of the affirmations means in more depth.

I love you.

This is about your spirit and the essence of who you are. Until we love ourselves, we cannot know love. If we do not have love within us, we have nothing to give others. It is impossible to give away something we do not possess. When we acknowledge ourselves and embrace who we are, then we can give. Even if you don't believe it now, keep saying "*I love you*" until you do.

I love my body.

This addresses the physical body. It isn't about our physical appearance or our self-criticisms about how we look. Without our bodies we can't experience anything, so we honor them for giving us the ability to experience life to the fullest. The body is our beautiful, sensory vehicle that allows us to move and experience all our senses—sight, sound, touch, feel, and taste. With this affirmation, we quit believing we have a faulty body and focus on everything our bodies can do.

These next two affirmations address the mind and being truthful with others and ourselves.

I forgive myself for the thoughts I live by that do not help me.

We forgive ourselves for the thoughts we have accumulated from early ages that do not serve us. We willingly let go of outdated thinking that holds us back from experiencing all that we desire. We let go of these thoughts now and are grateful for it. As a result, we forgive our minds for dictating to us how our lives look and what they "should" be like.

I forgive others for their thoughts and allow them to think whatever they desire.

We allow others to have their thoughts, and we forgive others and ourselves for believing we "should" all have the same thoughts.

I trust myself to know who I am. I do what pleases me in all areas of my life.

Follow your heart, and do what you desire in your work, hobbies, service to others, etc. Balance what you think you "should" be doing with what totally pleases you. When we hear ourselves say "should," we are listening to someone else's voice telling us what to do from the outside, instead of listening to our own heart.

I live my life completely, and I am grateful for being here.

Live your life fully without holding back in fear. Be grateful for the earth, air, fire, and water that make it possible for you to exist in and enjoy life. Without the elements, your body would not have a place to be. You couldn't experience your senses or move around and have the amazing opportunity to do anything you desire with your life.

8

SUCCESS STORIES

NOW LET'S LOOK AT THREE real-life experiences using this simple system so you know what you might expect.

Kyra, twenty-eight years old, said these affirmations two times a day for seven days. The first thing she noticed was that she set better boundaries. She wasn't doing what she thought she "should" as much. Instead, Kyra asked herself if it pleased her to do the activity, or if she was doing it out of obligation, a need to please someone else or to be liked. She really started looking more closely at her schedule. As a result, her life felt more balanced. She experienced a great deal of peace. Kyra particularly embraced the affirmation *I trust myself to know who I am*. She felt it was very profound. The thought *I love my body* was a challenge at first, but she integrated it with the thought that her body is what it is today, and she's grateful for it. She felt empowered in her life in every way, most noticeably in the area of her work. She felt less bothered by superficial things and overall felt much happier and more content, and she had more faith that things would work out for her.

June, sixty-five years old, said the affirmations once daily for ten days. She felt it gave her a great start to her day. It reinforced the idea of positive thinking. The affirmations reminded her to be grateful for all the good things in her life and put her in a good mood for the day. They reversed her negative thinking. They reminded her of her mother saying to her when she was having a hard time, "You are God's child; put your hand in God's and no harm will come to you." They gave her the same feeling of comfort she had when her mother used to say that to her. The process helped her readjust her thinking. She said if there was one word to describe her experience, it would be *inspiring*.

Tiana, forty-four years old, said her affirmations three times daily for ten days. She felt increased confidence in herself. She noticed a strong gravitation to the things she used to do and enjoy: listening to music, being in nature, moving her body to music in swimming and dancing. Every few days she felt a different resonance with an affirmation. The first was "I love you." The next was "I'm grateful to be here." She felt more accepting of herself and had more appreciation and gratitude for her daily life, even for the mundane things that used to irritate her. She realized how lucky she is to have everything she has. She became more insightful, experiencing greater awareness of herself and others. She found herself laughing more and was less critical and judgmental of herself. She felt much less fearful of life.

9

OTHER IDEAS THAT MAY HELP

HERE ARE SOME ALTERNATIVE WAYS to think about our physical bodies, feeling worthy, living a balanced life, and romantic relationships.

The Body

We have come to view the body as an object. We're unhappy with it because it's not the correct shape, height, or weight. Instead of thinking about how your body looks, focus on what it does for you. Be grateful for your body and its function and health. You would have no life and no experience without it.

Take good care of your body. Melt into the water, consume the air, bask in a fire's glow, and honor the earth you stand upon and are made from. Your body gives you the ability to walk, run, taste, feel, touch, hear and see. How else would we experience the rejuvenating properties of water, its taste, fluidity, sound or the beauty of the sun reflecting on it? Our body gives us the opportunity to experience all we desire in life. What could be grander?

Commitment

One reason we have trouble committing to ourselves is that we believe there is something we have done to become unworthy, and there must be something we can do to become worthy. The truth is that we are worthy. The spirit we are is and always has been worthy. We are worthy, *period.*

Living a balanced life

When we balance our physical, emotional, mental, and spiritual lives, we feel more content and satisfied with what we're doing. Ask yourself these questions and see where you can improve the quality of your life.

- Am I taking good care of my body?
- Do I pay attention to my health, diet, sleep schedule, and regular exercise?
- Am I taking care of my emotional needs?
- Am I acknowledging my feelings?

- Do I provide quiet time to nourish my soul?
- Do I quiet my mind and allow my intuitive self to come through?

Opening the heart

When we meet a potential partner and have a thrilling connection with him or her, we think it will last forever. Both people are moving from their hearts, and it's beautiful. It feels so intoxicating.

We are all looking for an open-hearted connection. When we reach for this golden ring and finally get what we've longed for, we want to take it home and keep it forever. We want to imagine how it will turn out, and we believe it will always stay the same.

We can't know if a relationship will stay open or not. One of us, or both, could close down and return to our old comfort zone. One of us could change our mind and become uncomfortable about being in a vulnerable position. When this happens, we feel confused. How could these great feelings change? We feel tricked. We no longer trust ourselves to know the truth we thought we saw.

Well, we can't know the outcome of any relationship. There are too many factors involved. We don't know if we are open enough to maintain such an open-hearted relationship or if the other person is able to do so. All we can do is enjoy the wonder of each moment we are in. Tell the truth of how you feel in each moment, relish each feeling as it occurs, and allow the relationship to be how it is in that very instant. We can't tell how we will feel tomorrow, but we can hold the intention to have an open-hearted connection in our life.

Simple works!

You might wonder how such a simple system of saying specific affirmations can change how you feel about your life in just a few days. I know from my personal journey and sharing this system with others that it *can* make a real difference, changing our thoughts and feelings. You only have good things to experience by doing it. I wish you well.

10

THE SIX BASICS

IN THIS SECTION, YOU WILL find six foundational statements you may use to prepare for moving on to using the more specific statements for forgiveness and thanks in advance that follow.

Choose a statement that resonates with you. Work with one at a time. Letting them integrate in one at a time is a way to shift and balance your system, giving you a great foundation from which to springboard on to more specific things you would like to delete and change.

Center yourself. You can direct your requests to your higher self, Source, God, the Universe, your angels—whomever you feel comfortable asking.

Doing one at a time, write each statement on sticky notes and place them where you will see them several times a day to input it into your system. The time it takes to integrate it into your system will vary. I knew I was ready to move on to the next foundational statement when I stopped noticing the sticky note affirmation. When you feel that the foundational statement you are working on has been integrated into your thinking, then move on to the next one, until you have completed all six.

1. Thanks in advance for deleting and letting go of all the thoughts and ideas that do not serve me.
2. Thanks in advance for bringing in all the thoughts and ideas that will assist me on my path.
3. Thanks in advance for grounding me and attaching my ethereal (spiritual) body to my physical body.
4. Thanks in advance for calming down my central nervous system and letting go of any anxiety I may be experiencing.
5. Thanks in advance for balancing my mental, emotional, and physical bodies.
6. Thanks in advance for helping me to remember who I am and who everyone else is.

11

FORGIVING A PERSON

NOW WE CAN MOVE ON to specific items we would like to delete from our system.

Choose a specific person whom you have a hard time forgiving. Think about that person and the situation you would like to release. Close your eyes and feel into what bothers you about it. Write out all that comes to you. Forgive yourself for your perceptions, and forgive the transgressor for their part in the situation.

Following is an example of the two-step process for forgiving a father.

Step 1

I forgive my father for abandoning me.
I forgive myself for believing my father should have
    been there for me.

I forgive my father for being selfish.

I forgive myself for believing my life should have been
different from what it is.

I forgive myself for all the years I harbored resentment
around this. The decisions he made had nothing to
do with me.

I forgive myself for believing that I did something to
cause this.

You can keep writing out your list of "I forgive"
statements until you feel like it's completed for this
circumstance, and then go to the next step.

Step 2

A way to bring in a new thought around this subject
is to write down:

> Thanks in advance for assisting me
> in letting go of any negative thoughts
> I have formed around my relationship
> with my father.

Again, use sticky notes and place the new thought
around where you will see it multiple times per day until
it becomes your thought!

12

HOW TO PROCEED

WHEN THERE IS A PROBLEM with a coworker, family member, spouse, relationship, or situation you find you can't stop thinking about, that's the time to use this system. You will be able to let go of the thoughts you are clinging to and remedy the situation.

Feel into the situation and write down what is bothering you about it. Make a list of all the conflicting emotions you are feeling, how you feel about your reaction to the situation, and what upsets you about the other people involved. Take that information and start writing out forgiveness statements. Forgive yourself for your part, and forgive the other people involved. Forgive yourself for your expectations and the expectations of other people.

When you find yourself having ruminating thoughts about yourself—your weight, appearance, intelligence, health, abundance, lack, anxiety, obsession, addiction, illness, inabilities—write them down and start the forgiveness statements. When you notice thoughts during the day that keep repeating, jot them down and work off your list one at a time.

At first it may feel daunting to come up with the statements to forgive, so in the next section I am offering some prompts.

13

STEP 1: FORGIVING YOURSELF

IT MAY BE EASIER AT first to choose from a list of prompts toward self-forgiveness. Here are 100 examples to choose from. Use the ones that feel true for you.

After you write out the forgiveness statement for a given topic, go to the next chapter to select a "Thanks in advance for …" statement to write on your sticky notes. Again, complete one situation at a time.

I forgive myself for …

1. believing lies and feeling betrayed.
2. wanting to punish others who have hurt me.
3. being so angry I see red and wanting to cause someone harm.
4. taking things personally.

5. believing that if someone really loved me, they would act in a different way from what they do.
6. not setting boundaries.
7. believing that I can't feel angry and that others should never feel angry towards me.
8. believing that it's my fault when someone is angry with me and that I have to fix it.
9. believing that when I feel angry, it's someone else's fault.
10. compulsively wanting to help other people.
11. saying yes to things I don't want to do.
12. not knowing what I want or need.
13. pleasing others instead of pleasing myself.
14. being attracted to needy people.
15. blaming others for my feelings and struggles.
16. creating unhealthy patterns.
17. feeling artificially good about myself when I am helping others.
18. being mean to myself and hating myself.
19. being rigid and controlling.
20. worrying excessively about things small and large.
21. losing sleep worrying about other people's problems.
22. going to extreme lengths to control others.
23. feeling depressed and unmotivated.
24. trying to control events and people using helplessness, guilt, coercion, threats, advice-giving, manipulation, or domination.
25. pretending things aren't as bad as they are.

26. desperately seeking love and approval from unavailable people.
27. pushing into relationships without considering whether it's a good situation for me.
28. losing interest in my own life while in a relationship.
29. saying only what I thought another person wanted to hear *(you may replace "another person" with the name)*.
30. allowing other people's emotions to control me.
31. believing that a relationship has to be hard.
32. putting others before myself.
33. having unhealthy boundaries.
34. thinking I know what is best for other people.
35. believing that another person feels the same way I do *(or replace "another person" with the name)*.
36. not trusting that I know what is best for me.
37. the expectations I made up about a particular relationship.
38. giving all my thoughts and energy away to another person.
39. believing that I am nothing if I'm not loved by someone else.
40. believing that another person *(or use name)* is not giving me the attention I think I need.
41. believing the illusion I created around a particular relationship.
42. allowing others to cross my boundaries.
43. not loving myself.
44. engaging in a harmful relationship.

45. allowing others to make decisions for me.
46. expecting perfection of myself and others.
47. having contempt for myself.
48. acting in irrational ways.
49. being angry.
50. pushing my needs and people away.
51. trying to control people and outcomes.
52. believing others cannot take care of themselves.
53. not speaking my truth.
54. not standing my ground.
55. resisting change.
56. perpetuating unhealthy learned behaviors.
57. thinking my way is the only way.
58. not taking care of me.
59. enabling others.
60. rescuing others.
61. Finding fault in others.
62. being unable to say no.
63. feeling compelled to help others.
64. not communicating and confronting people's behaviors that are affecting me.
65. feeling guilt and shame.
66. feeling like I am not enough.
67. being codependent.
68. feeling unsafe.
69. feeling powerless.
70. viewing my life through what someone else thinks is good for me.
71. not having a sense of myself and who I am.

72. needing something outside myself to define my identity.

73. needing a relationship to feel like I am worthy.

74. participating in toxic relationships.

75. recreating my childhood experiences by engaging in similarly patterned relationships in adulthood.

76. being attached to something outside myself.

77. participating in one-way relationships.

78. not knowing what my needs are.

79. believing someone will save me from whatever I feel I need to be saved from and being willing to give up myself to be saved.

80. always taking care of someone or something else.

81. allowing my sense of self to come from attaching to someone else and disowning my own self.

82. being wishy washy.

83. blaming my dysfunction on other people.

84. believing that I am not enough.

85. looking outside myself for validation.

86. feeling unworthy.

87. believing that I did anything wrong in this situation.

88. not valuing myself.

89. feeling guilty about not giving myself away to other people and situations.

90. wanting to control and manipulate to get what I think I need.

91. not taking responsibility for myself and my well being.
92. believing I am responsible for other people or things that are out of my control.
93. believing that anger and emotions are bad.
94. seeking validation.
95. begging for approval.
96. over-explaining.
97. not recognizing when I am seeking my own sense of self and validation from other people.
98. giving myself away.
99. imagining someone's watching me and approving of what I look like and what I am doing.
100. being human.

14

STEP 2: THANKS IN ADVANCE

NOW THAT YOU HAVE MADE your forgiveness statement regarding a situation, create or select a "Thanks in advance for" statement. Write them on sticky notes and display them where you will see it. Here are fifty prompts to get you started.

Thanks in advance for ...

1. setting limits on what I will do for people.
2. setting limits on what I will allow people to do to me.
3. nurturing myself and taking care of my needs first.
4. having a great functioning body that allows me to do all the things I desire to do.

5. doing healthy things for my physical, emotional, mental and spiritual well-being.
6. learning to be kind to myself.
7. detaching from unhealthy relationships and attaching to my own wellbeing.
8. helping when I can, and letting go when I can't help.
9. allowing others to experience the consequences of their actions and bear the responsibility of their own life and choices.
10. living my own life.
11. surrendering to what is and allowing everything to be as it is.
12. letting go of past regrets and fears.
13. choosing not to try to control and micro-manage.
14. letting go of people who no longer are a positive match for me.
15. recognizing that it is OK to feel angry and for others to express their anger without it being the end of the world.
16. validating my feelings.
17. taking responsibility for my life, feelings, and worth.
18. releasing guilt from my past creations that I thought were helping me.
19. detaching from unhealthy people and situations so I can focus on myself.
20. being responsible for myself and allowing others to be responsible for themselves.
21. assisting me in observing my feelings.

22. being kind and forgiving.
23. having healthy boundaries.
24. loving and accepting myself and others.
25. engaging in healthy relationships.
26. doing my best in all circumstances.
27. always choosing what is best for me.
28. being gentle and easy with myself.
29. being patient and trusting that all is unfolding in the best way for my highest good.
30. calming down my obsessive programing.
31. standing in my own personal power.
32. going with the flow and trusting all is unfolding in the best possible way.
33. seeing clearly with compassion, wisdom and understanding.
34. loving and accepting myself and others for who we are.
35. setting healthy boundaries and only doing what pleases me.
36. creating a life of ease and beauty.
37. assisting me in bringing in all that I am asking for.
38. seeing myself through my own eyes and not through someone else's eyes.
39. letting go of focusing on others instead of myself.
40. living my life for me.
41. recognizing when I am in other people's business and not focusing on my own business.
42. setting boundaries and sticking to them.

43. understanding that anger is a valid emotion.
44. prioritizing me.
45. knowing what I want and need.
46. remembering that we are all responsible for our own well-being.
47. being able to say "no thanks" when I don't want to do something.
48. knowing that I am worthy.
49. creating healthy relationships.
50. knowing that I am loveable.

15

FORGIVING OTHERS

HERE ARE SOME FORGIVENESS STATEMENTS to get you started on forgiving others. Fill in the blank with the name of the person you want to forgive.

I forgive _____ for not acting the way I want them to.

I forgive _____ for turning this around on me.

I forgive _____ for not seeing things the same way I do.

I forgive any people associated with this situation.

I forgive _____ for being the self they have been conditioned to be.

I forgive _____ for aligning with _____ and rejecting me and talking bad about me to their friends.

I forgive _____ for attacking my integrity.

I forgive _____ for any future harm they may cause me.

_____ is welcome to live their life however they choose.

_____ doesn't need to conform to my way of thinking.

_____ can believe anything they think about me.

_____ can be shocked and upset.

_____ can believe that I am the enemy.

_____ can reject the help I offered.

_____ can coerce friends into being loyal to them and rejecting me.

_____ can believe that I am a bad person.

16

TWO STATEMENTS

HERE ARE TWO MORE EXAMPLES of statements you might put together in following the two steps.

Example 1

Step 1

I forgive _____ for being their conditioned self. I forgive myself for believing they should be different from what they are. They are welcome to live their life however they choose to. They don't need to conform to my way of thinking. They can be shocked and upset. They can believe that I am the enemy. They can be in denial and not take responsibility for their actions.

Step 2

Thanks in advance for allowing _____ to be exactly how they are and to have their own perspective.

Example 2

Step 1

I forgive myself for being unkind to the customer service representative I spoke with today that came from my own frustration at the amount of time I spent trying to get the issue resolved. I forgive the customer service representative for not being able to help me efficiently. I forgive myself for any negative ideas I had prior to making the call. I forgive myself for believing this situation should have been different from what it was. I forgive myself for overreacting in this situation.

Step 2

Thanks in advance for being calm and peaceful when things don't go the way I think they should.

17

FOR THOSE ON A SPIRITUAL PATH

HERE ARE SOME ADVANCED STATEMENTS to use if they resonate with you. They are very helpful in raising our vibration and the vibration of the planet. Choose what resonates with you and work one at a time, using the sticky notes as reminders.

Thanks in advance for ...

- opening to receive the Cosmic Mother.
- knowing what nourishes me.
- knowing what refuels my body.
- knowing what is nectar to my soul.
- knowing what brings me back to life.

- knowing who my tribe is and knowing how to access the beings that will benefit from my wisdom.
- lighting up the world.
- embracing the unique light I came to share.
- treating my time on earth as a glorious vacation.
- dreaming a new world into being.
- unlimited funds.
- ease, peace, love, fun, beauty, and youthfulness.
- being a reflection of my best and healthiest self.
- appearing as if I'm in my prime.
- my car working perfectly.
- approving of myself.
- being wise.
- being strong.
- being competent.
- being kind and forgiving.
- taking care of my body.
- engaging in healthy activities.
- eating heathy food.
- being my perfect weight.
- having healthy boundaries.
- being a good friend.
- being grateful for my life.
- loving and accepting myself and others.
- engaging in healthy relationships.
- being intelligent.
- being worthy.
- being aware of my thoughts.
- doing my best in all circumstances.

- being in balance.
- my energy centers running clear.
- having all that I need and desire.
- loving my work.
- always choosing what is best for me.
- being the great "I Am."
- knowing that everything flows to me in a simple, easy and fun way.
- being gentle and easy with myself.
- being patient and trusting that all is unfolding in the best way for my best and highest good.
- knowing the Universe has me covered in all ways.
- for calming down my obsessive programing.

18

ASCENSION, LIGHTWORKERS, AND ADVANCED IDEAS

THIS SECTION OFFERS MORE ADVANCED statements that are spiritual concepts and some that have a global impact. Choose what resonates with you.

I forgive ...

- mass consciousness for believing that we have created negativity and transmute the negativity by forgiving it all.
- myself and others for believing that we age.
- myself and others for believing in increased pain and health problems as we age.
- myself for having limiting thoughts.

Thanks in advance for ...

- being free to be who I am.
- knowing that I am the great "I Am."
- all abundance.
- being the all in all.
- knowing that I am here to bring light into the world and to exponentially radiate the highest vibration possible in this realm.
- knowing that I am God incarnate.
- standing in my own personal power.
- going with the flow and trusting all is unfolding in the best possible way.
- embodying and radiating out our original idea of what we intended this world to be.
- knowing who I am and who each of us is.
- knowing that we are all extensions of Source and we have the ability to create freely.
- being here at this time, assisting humanity in raising the vibration of the earth and each and every one of us.
- knowing that I am love.
- seeing clearly with compassion, wisdom and understanding.
- understanding and knowing that we are creating all the experiences that we are experiencing in every moment.
- taking care of my physical, emotional, and mental bodies.
- being in balance.

- knowing that nothing matters because it's all made up, even spirituality.
- being in perfect health.
- loving and accepting myself and others for who we are.
- being compassionate toward all sentient beings.
- setting healthy boundaries and doing only what pleases me.
- opening to receive the information and guidance from the highest beings of love and light to share what is best for us in the earth plane.
- realizing and seeing the god in myself and in others.
- us collectively supporting the environment in healthy, conscious ways in word and deed.
- waking up and creating ways to support the health of the earth and all beings upon her.
- dispelling aging.
- ease in knowing what to share with humanity, the planet, and the people.
- creating a life of ease and beauty.
- creating what makes me feel abundant and overspilling with life.
- for deleting the thoughts and ideas I have created that no longer help me to live the life I desire.
- assisting me in bringing in all that I am asking for.
- aligning with the perfect original blueprint of all of my bodies.
- creating monetary abundance with ease.

19

LIFE REVIEW

A LIFE REVIEW IS ANOTHER ADVANCED idea that may interest you if you desire to let go of as much as you can while you are in this world.

When we transition out of the body, we see a recap of all the times we were kind or unkind in this lifetime, as well as which goals we accomplished and which ones we didn't quite make. Then we use that information to decide what we want to learn next time we incarnate, should we choose to do that again. If periodically we forgive ourselves for when we have been unkind, consciously or unconsciously, that forgiveness could be helpful in our soul's evolution. It won't cost much to try!

Example 1

Step 1

I forgive myself for all the times in the past when I have been less than kind. I forgive myself for giving in to frustration when it feels like things are going against my will. I forgive myself for believing that things should always be easy and work according to my plans. I forgive those I have blamed for my misguided thoughts and ideas. I take responsibility for all my own reactions. I go with the flow and I am able to be gracious under pressure.

Step 2

Thanks in advance for allowing things to be the way they are and not how I think they "should" be.

Example 2

Step 1

I forgive myself for all my misguided thoughts and ideas. I forgive myself for believing others should think and feel the way I do. I allow all beings to believe whatever they want to. I accept that we are all living our lives to the best of our abilities, according to the information we have accumulated along the way. My thoughts and ideas are best for me and me alone. I control my own universe and allow others to control theirs. I forgive myself for any and all unkindness I have exhibited, knowingly and unknowingly.

Step 2

Thanks in advance for being kind and compassionate to myself and others in all situations.

20

WHERE DO YOU GO FROM HERE?

NOW THAT YOU HAVE LET go of and cleared out your body, mind, and spirit, what's next? How do you operate in your whole freedom from the limiting thoughts you have now released?

When I read Melody Beattie's book *Codependent No More*, I was fearful that I would forget the principles I had learned. I decided to read an excerpt from one of her other books every day for a year to reinforce what I had read and learned. I chose *The Language of Letting Go*. I encourage you to choose something inspiring to you. It's a great way to keep yourself tuned in to your new way of being on your journey!

Do some kind of practice at the beginning and end of your day to stay focused on your journey to freedom. Listen to uplifting podcasts, read any books that resonate with you, hang out with positive people—whatever keeps you moving forward toward the life you desire. Take at least half an hour a day to do nothing and just be. Meditate if that works for you. Take baths, go for a walk with no destination in mind, read inspirational material, and make sure you are focused on your wellbeing in all of you, mind, body and spirit. Take excellent care of your body.

When we start changing the way we think and the ways the mind tries to protect the body, we may have thoughts that we are a little "crazy." When we start thinking outside the box, it's new and exciting. However, some people and relatives may be confused and fearful of the new you. This is when to remember that everyone is welcome to their own thoughts and ideas, and we are also entitled to our own new way of thinking. Sometimes we may feel alone or like an outsider, but these are fleeting moments, and we aren't here to convince anyone else that our way is correct and theirs is faulty. We need to show grace to ourselves and others by standing our ground but also by guiding conversations to comfortable topics. Those around you may or may not notice how happy you are, but it's not up to you to convince others of your peace—they will notice or not.

As you change, your friends and interests will change too. What and who was interesting to you before will evolve. Don't worry—as you change, your old friends will not be as interested in the friendship either, and they will want to move on too.

Occasionally I would be transforming a particularly difficult pattern, and in my irritation I would have fleeting thoughts of quitting. This is a normal reaction, so just keep on going. If your mind tries to tell you, "If you let this go, you won't have anything to live for," ignore it. Sometimes the mind is a liar and is only protecting itself. It doesn't want to let go of an entrenched idea, but I promise you there is only peace on the other side. Keep going!

Search out whatever resonates with you, and keep adding to your freedom and openness and enjoy your life!

Recommended Reading

I AM ADDING A RECOMMENDED BOOK list you can peruse and of course you can find what resonates with you to further you on your path of discovery. Just keep on going with your new-found freedom.

Codependent no More
Beyond Codependency
The Language of Letting Go
Stop Being Mean to Yourself
Melody Beattie

The Emotion Code
Dr. Bradley Nelson

The Power of Now
Eckhart Tolle

Conversations with God 1–3
Neale Donald-Walsh

Anatomy of the Spirit
Energy Anatomy
Carolyn Myss

You Can Heal Your Life
Heal your Body
Louise L. Hay

Loving What Is
Byron Katie

Many Lives, Many Masters
Messages from the Masters
Brian L Weiss, MD

A Mythic Life
Jump Time
Jean Houston

Hands of Light
Light Emerging
Barbara Ann Brennan

The Isaiah Effect
Wisdom Codes
Beyond Zero Point
The Lost Mode of Prayer
The Gift of the Blessing
Gregg Braden

The Hero's Journey
The Power of Myth
Joseph Campbell

Essential Reiki
Diane Stein

Woman Who Glows in the Dark
Elena Avila

Passage Meditation
Eknath Easwaran

The Four Agreements
Miguel Ruiz

The Power of Now
Eckhart Tolle

Christ Mind series
Paul Ferrini

Your Aura and Your Chakras
Karla McLaren

Becoming Supernatural
Dr. Joe Dispenza

The Zahir
The Alchemist
Paulo Coelho

The Wisdom of the Enneagram
Don Richard Riso/Russ Hudson

Power vs. Force
Dr. David R. Hawkins

Be Here Now
Ram Das

A Course in Miracles
Dr. Helen Schucman

Living a Course in Miracles
Jon Mundy, PhD

A Return to Love
Marianne Williamson

Shaman, Healer, Sage
Alberto Villoldo, PhD

The Worthy Mind
Meadow DeVor

Braiding Sweetgrass
Robin Wall Kimerer

Other authors I have read and recommend:

Deepak Chopra
Nassim Haramein
The Dalai Lama
Wayne Dyer
Dolores Cannon
Sonia Choquette
David Deida
Alan Watts
Thich Nhat Hanh
Sylvia Brown
James Van Praagh
Cyndi Dale
Josc Silva

Journal

Use the following pages to journal your way through the two-step process.

Step 1: I forgive myself for ...

Step 2: Thanks in advance for …

Step 1: I forgive myself for ...

Step 2: Thanks in advance for ...

Step 1: I forgive myself for ...

Step 2: Thanks in advance for ...

Step 1: I forgive myself for ...

Step 2: Thanks in advance for ...

Step 1: I forgive myself for ...

Step 2: Thanks in advance for ...

Step 1: I forgive myself for ...

Step 2: Thanks in advance for ...

Step 1: I forgive myself for ...

Step 2: Thanks in advance for ...

Step 1: I forgive myself for ...

Step 2: Thanks in advance for ...

Step 1: I forgive myself for ...

Printed in the United States
by Baker & Taylor Publisher Services